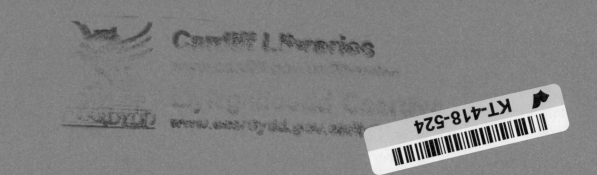

THE STORY OF THE VIKINGS

PICTURE BOOK

Megan Cullis

Illustrated by Giorgio Bacchin

Designed by Stephen Moncrieff,
Emily Barden & Samantha Barrett

Expert advice by Sue Brunning, Institute of Archaeology,
University College London

CONTENTS

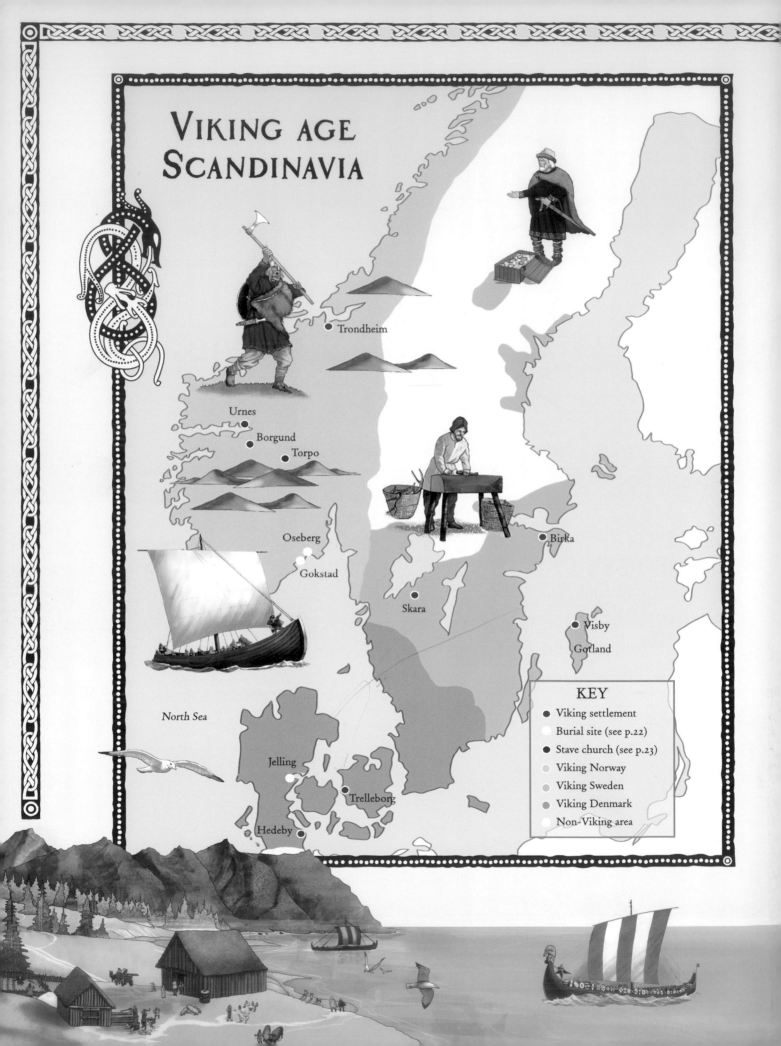

VIKING AGE SCANDINAVIA

Trondheim

Urnes

Borgund

Torpo

Oseberg

Gokstad

Birka

Skara

Visby

Gotland

North Sea

Jelling

Trelleborg

Hedeby

KEY

- ● Viking settlement
- ○ Burial site (see p.22)
- ● Stave church (see p.23)
- Viking Norway
- Viking Sweden
- Viking Denmark
- Non-Viking area

THE VIKINGS

Around 1,200 years ago, bands of seaborne raiders began terrorizing coastal settlements around Europe. These fearsome warriors from Scandinavia, in northern Europe, became known as Vikings.

> "The raiding of heathen men miserably devastated God's church in Lindisfarne island by looting and slaughter."

An English monk describes a Viking raid on England, in a book called *The Anglo Saxon Chronicles*, written in the 800s.

Viking raiders often struck under the cover of darkness. They rowed up rivers or landed on sloping beaches, before plundering settlements, looting for treasure. Then, they sailed home.

Some experts believe that Viking ships were decorated with ferocious-looking dragon heads, like this.

But the Vikings weren't just raiders. From around the 850s, they began to conquer and settle in new lands, where they lived as merchants, farmers and craft workers.

Beautifully crafted Viking objects have survived to this day, such as this splendid gold and silver brooch. It was made by a Viking metal worker.

VIKING SHIPS

The Vikings were masters of the seas. They built all kinds of ships, from warships designed for swift raids to cargo ships capable of carrying heavy loads across vast expanses of water.

LONGSHIPS

Viking warships, known as longships, would have looked spectacular. With a long, sleek design, they were narrow enough to be rowed up rivers and light enough to be carried across land.

Carved, wooden dragon heads are thought to have been attached to a longship's front, to strike fear into people as the ship approached.

Bronze weather vanes, like this, were fitted on the front of a longship to help show sailors the direction of the wind. They were probably hung with bright streamers that rippled in the breeze.

Viking ships were built from overlapping planks of wood riveted together. This made them flexible and watertight.

Shields were likely to have been hung along the sides of longships to keep them out of the way.

Ships were moored using large, heavy anchors. This Viking anchor is made from stone wedged into a wooden frame, and is nearly 1m (3ft) across.

In 1880, this Viking ship was discovered at Oseberg in Norway. The remains of a Viking woman were found with the ship. Important people, such as warriors or rulers, were often buried inside ships when they died.

Mast

Square sail
strengthened with
strips of cloth

This picture was painted around the year
1100. It shows Viking warriors rowing
towards Britain in a fleet of longships.

Large oar
for steering

Food and water for
the journey were
carried at the back
of the ship.

CARGO SHIPS

Viking cargo ships were called knarrs.
Wider, deeper and slower than longships,
they were built for transporting
goods over long distances.

Knarrs were designed with
a large pit in the middle for
live animals, textiles and
other trading goods.

This Viking coin probably
shows a *knarr*, though its
shape has been simplified
by the maker.

5

BATTLE GEAR

Viking warriors were fierce and deadly fighters.
Armed with helmets, shields and an array of fearsome
weapons, they crushed resistance all over Europe.

SWORDS

Viking swords were highly prized and
often passed down from father to son.
Warriors sometimes gave them
ferocious-sounding names, such
as *Leg-biter* or *Adder*.

This is a real Viking sword,
made in around 900.

Viking long
axes looked
like this.

AXES

Every Viking warrior had a couple
of axes. Their blades were made
from iron and could inflict
terrible wounds.

Long axes were
swung with
both hands.

Small axes
could be
thrown.

This warrior's sword has two
sharp edges for slashing.

Small axes like this could
be hidden under cloaks
for surprise attacks.

SAXES

Most warriors owned a
sharp knife, called
a *sax*.

A *sax* was carried in a leather and wooden holder, called
a scabbard, which could be hung from a warrior's belt.
These are copies of a Viking *sax* and scabbard.

SHIELDS

Most warriors carried a wooden shield, painted with bright, eye-catching patterns. A metal dome in the middle, called a *boss*, protected the warrior's hand.

HORSES

Viking horses were small and used mainly to transport warriors to a battlefield before they dismounted to fight. From around 1100, some military leaders rode into battle and fought on horseback.

This tapestry, from around 1190, shows a warrior riding a horse into battle. He carries a kite-shaped shield, specially designed for fighting on horseback.

HELMETS

Helmets were made of iron or hardened leather. A few had eye guards, but these were probably only worn by important warriors.

Most Vikings wore simple helmets like this reconstructed copy, with a pointed top and a straight nosepiece.

This battered helmet, found in Norway, is the only surviving Viking helmet. Its protective eye 'spectacles' would have looked terrifying in battle.

Mail, made of small interlocking iron rings, was sometimes attached to a helmet to protect the warrior's neck.

THE VIKING WORLD

The Vikings explored far and wide. They reached as far as North America in the West, and the cities of Baghdad and Constantinople in the East. Many went to trade, some went to conquer and others settled peacefully among the locals.

Turf house

Viking explorer Erik the Red founded Brattahlid, in Greenland, in 985. Although it was cold and icy, he named the island 'Greenland' to encourage other Vikings to settle there.

In the 870s, Vikings settled on an island which they named Iceland, after its ice-covered lakes. The place where they settled became known as Reykjavik. It was so cold that they covered their houses in turf, to help keep the heat in.

Reykjavik
ICELAND

GREENLAND

Brattahlid

ATLANTIC OCEAN

SCOTLAND

Viking raiders first invaded Ireland in the 790s, attacking monasteries and looting treasure.

Dublin

York

IRELAND

ENGLAND

Viking explorers reached Newfoundland, in North America, in around the year 1000. They named it 'Vinland', which may have meant 'wine land', after the grapes that were said to grow there.

L'Anse aux Meadows

NEWFOUNDLAND

In 911, Vikings gained control of an area that became known as Normandy. The name came from a word meaning 'Norseman', another term for a Viking.

Normandy

FRANCE

TRANSPORT

When they weren't using boats or ships, Vikings rode on horseback, walked, skied or ice skated. They transported heavy loads in horse-drawn wooden vehicles, such as wagons or sleds.

During the cold winter months, Vikings sped across hard snow and frozen rivers using sleds.

SPAIN

Cordoba

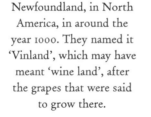

There weren't many proper roads in Scandinavia. Carts like this one were pulled along rough paths, but this was hard work, so they weren't widely used.

Viking sailors navigated by watching the movements of fish and birds.

KEY

Viking homelands

Under Viking control from the 700s

Under Viking control from the 800s

Under Viking control from the 900s

Under Viking control from the 1000s

Viking routes

Rivers   Cities

The place names in bold are modern names.

To get between rivers, Vikings carried their boats, or rolled them along the ground on logs.

Staraja Ladoga

Birka

Novgorod

Bulghar

Fleets of longships sailed down the River Volga to the port of Itil, where the Vikings traded furs and slaves for Arab silver.

River Volga

In around 1011, Vladimir the Great – a prince of Viking origin – built St. Sophia Cathedral in Kiev.

Vikings settled in what is now Russia in around 860. The native peoples, the Slavs, called the Vikings 'Rus', meaning 'men who row'. The name 'Russia' probably comes from the word 'Rus'.

Kiev

Itil

RUSSIA

A Rus merchant

BLACK SEA

CASPIAN SEA

Constantinople

ITALY

Viking merchants rode on camels across the desert to Baghdad, where they exchanged goods for silver coins, spices and silk.

Baghdad

MEDITERRANEAN SEA

Some Viking warriors settled in Constantinople, the capital of the great Byzantine Empire, where they acted as bodyguards to the emperor. They became known as Varangian Guards.

RTH AFRICA

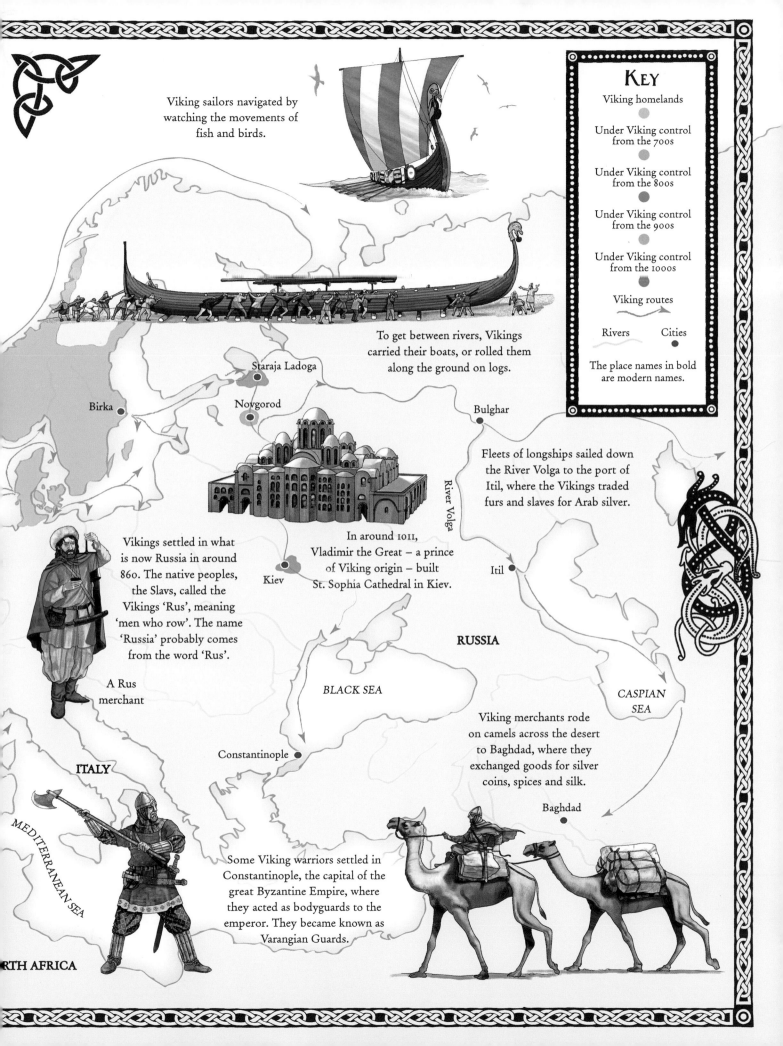

At Home

Despite their warlike reputation, most Vikings enjoyed a simple, peaceful life at home. They worked as farmers, fishermen and craft workers, and lived in big wooden homes, called longhouses.

A longhouse usually had just one big room, where everyone slept, ate and worked together.

Thatched roof

Animal enclosure

Smoke hole

Storehouse

Wooden bench

Loom for weaving cloth

Cooking and eating

Viking families ate two large meals a day – one in the morning, and another at night, after the day's work was finished. Food was cooked in pots over a fire in the middle of the longhouse.

Drinks such as ale or mead (a kind of honey wine) were served in hollow animal horns, like this one.

Large iron cauldrons like these were used to boil hearty meat stews and vegetable soups.

During feasts, the Vikings raised their horns to toast each other's health and happiness.

BED TIME

Longhouses were always bustling with activity, so there wasn't much room for furniture. While most people had to make do with wooden benches along the walls of the longhouse, wealthy landowners and their wives slept in beds.

This copy of a Viking bed has carved bedposts, designed in the shape of animal heads. Beds were probably lined with straw and soft animal skins.

KEEPING CLEAN

The Vikings took pride in their appearance, and washed regularly. Every Saturday, they washed in lakes, streams or bathhouses, before putting on freshly laundered clothes. They called Saturday *Laugardagr*, which means 'washing day' in their language, Old Norse.

Some experts think this whalebone board was used for smoothing and pleating cloth.

A round, heated lump of glass was used to press clothes flat, with the smoothing board underneath.

This Viking comb and case are made from deer antler. Combs were used to smooth long hair and beards, and to get rid of any dirt or lice.

ORNAMENTS

Rich Vikings loved to show off their wealth, and adorned themselves with glistening jewels, rows of polished beads and ornaments made from gold and silver.

BEADS

Wealthy women hung bright bead necklaces from their tunics. Small objects, such as keys, coins, tweezers or toothpicks, were sometimes hung from the necklaces, too.

Some of the finest bead necklaces were strung with exotic silver or gold coins.

These beads are made from glass, silver, amethyst (a purple rock mineral) and amber (hardened tree resin).

PINS AND BROOCHES

Men and women wore elaborate pins and brooches to fasten cloaks, tunics and shawls. They were often made from gold, silver or bronze, and finely decorated with intricate patterns.

These two pins are made of gold, covered with leaf and animal head patterns. Each pin is about the same width as a tennis ball.

Ring brooches could pierce through cloaks, tough animal hides and furs.

This silver ring brooch is decorated with punched designs.

RINGS

Many men and women wore gleaming gold and silver rings on their fingers, arms or necks.

This twisted gold arm ring has animal-shaped ends. It was worn around the wrist or on the upper arm.

Simple finger rings like this were made of one thin gold band, twisted around.

Arm rings were important to Viking rulers, and were given as gifts to reward loyal followers.

PENDANTS AND NECKLACES

Some people wore splendid necklaces and pendants around their necks. Pendants came in all shapes and sizes, but the most popular kinds were shaped like Viking gods or goddesses, and were worn as good luck charms to protect their owners.

Necklace designs were sometimes influenced by foreign styles. This Viking necklace is made from rock crystal mounted on silver. It is similar to Russian necklaces of the time.

This silver pendant is in the shape of Thor's hammer and decorated with a face. Thor was the Viking god of thunder (see pages 16-17).

TREASURE CHESTS

Many Vikings kept their jewels in chests, which were often just as beautiful as the jewels themselves. Some chests were originally made for use in churches and monasteries, and were stolen by Vikings during raids.

This is a copy of a Viking chest, made of gilt bronze and carved deer horn.

CRAFTS AND TRADE

As the Viking Age progressed, some settlements grew into prosperous trading towns. The streets were packed with bustling craft workers' workshops and market stalls, and merchants came from far and wide to sell their wares.

METALWORKING

Skilled Viking metal workers made all kinds of things, from iron nails and tools to lavish objects made out of silver, gold, pewter and bronze. Many were adorned with intricate patterns and animal motifs.

This iron blade is decorated with silver wire, shaped into a bird with a long, curly body.

Metal workers used heavy-duty iron tools, like these. Large shears were used to cut up hot pieces of iron, before they were shaped into objects such as padlocks or nails.

This is a busy Viking trading town. It's on the coast, making it easy for trading ships to sail in and out. Walls on the land side prevent raiders from looting the town's wealth and goods.

Wooden walkway

Market stall

Merchant ships full of cargo

BUYING AND SELLING

A few people in Viking towns used coins to pay for goods, but most people used scraps of silver, known as hacksilver, to exchange for goods instead.

Merchants carried scales with them to weigh out hacksilver.

Old silver ornaments were sometimes chopped up as hacksilver. This pile of real hacksilver is probably made up of cut-up arm rings.

GLASS

Glass was valuable, and used for making beautiful bowls, drinking cups and beads. Most glass was imported, but a few Viking craft workers made it themselves.

This green cup is made from blown glass. It was discovered in Birka, Sweden, but was probably imported from western Europe.

This Viking craftsman is blowing glass to make a drinking cup.

LEATHER GOODS

Leather workers treated animal skins to make tough, waterproof leather. They used the leather to make boots, money pouches and belts.

Workshops

Although these leather boots are over a thousand years old, you can still see the toggle fastenings on the sides.

15

VIKING RELIGION

The Vikings followed their own religion, which was filled with gods, goddesses and magical forces of nature. They believed the universe was divided into three levels. Gods and goddesses lived in a place called Asgard, at the top. Beneath Asgard was Earth, or Midgard, and below was the land of the dead, Niflheim.

An eagle roosted in the highest branches of Yggdrasil.

At the heart of the Viking universe was a magic ash tree, known as Yggdrasil.

A squirrel called Ratatoskr carried messages between the different levels.

ODIN

One-eyed Odin was the king of the gods, and the god of war. He started battles on Earth using a magic spear.

THOR

Thor was the fiery god of thunder and law. He wielded a powerful hammer and was immensely strong.

FREYA

Freya was Frey's twin sister, and the goddess of love and death. She rode through the sky in a chariot pulled by two great cats.

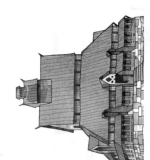

ASGARD

Each god or goddess lived in his or her own magnificent hall in Asgard.

FREY

Frey was god of fertility. He made the sun shine, the rain fall and the crops grow.

If a Viking warrior died in battle, he went to a glorious hall in Asgard, called Valhalla.

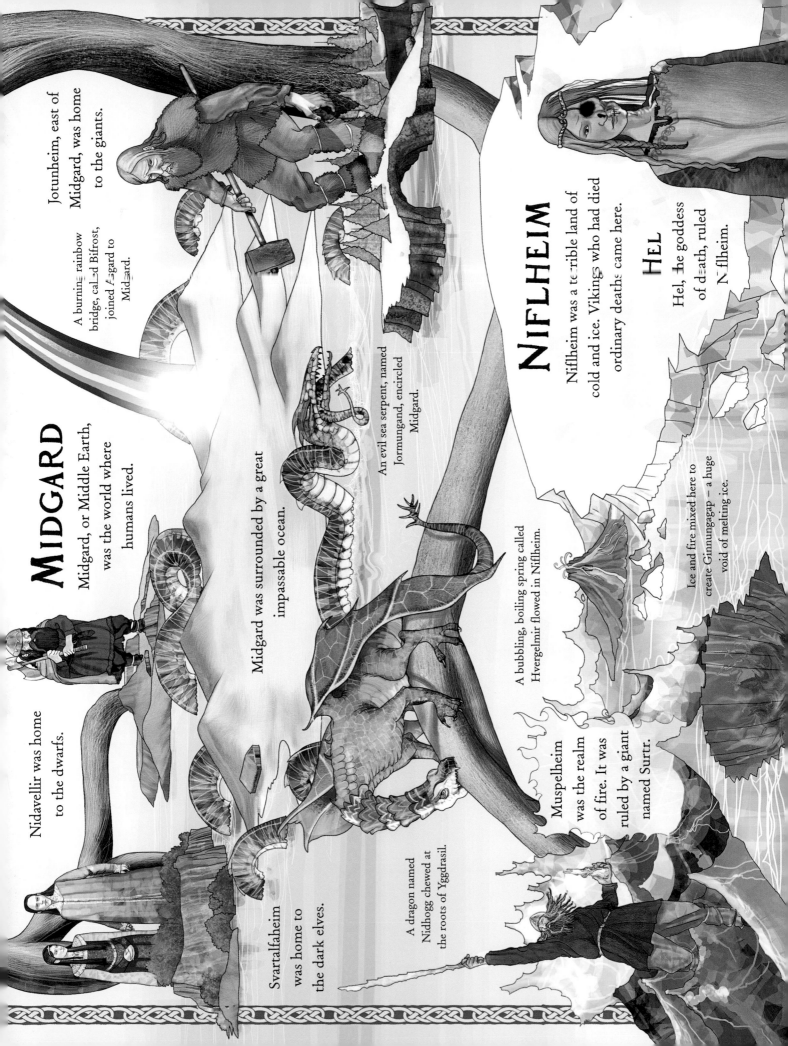

MIDGARD

Midgard, or Middle Earth, was the world where humans lived.

Jotunheim, east of Midgard, was home to the giants.

A burning rainbow bridge, called Bifrost, joined Asgard to Midgard.

Nidavellir was home to the dwarfs.

Midgard was surrounded by a great impassable ocean.

Svartalfaheim was home to the dark elves.

An evil sea serpent, named Jormungand, encircled Midgard.

A dragon named Nidhogg chewed at the roots of Yggdrasil.

NIFLHEIM

Niflheim was a terrible land of cold and ice. Vikings who had died ordinary deaths came here.

HEL

Hel, the goddess of death, ruled Niflheim.

A bubbling, boiling spring called Hvergelmir flowed in Niflheim.

Muspelheim was the realm of fire. It was ruled by a giant named Surtr.

Ice and fire mixed here to create Ginnungagap – a huge void of melting ice.

Pastimes

When work was over for the day, Viking families and friends gathered inside their homes to feast, listen to music and play games.

Feasting

The Vikings enjoyed grand feasts, especially during the cold, dark winters. Rich farmers held parties inside their longhouses, and entertained their guests with musicians and storytellers.

On special occasions, drinks were served in glass drinking cups, like this one.

Music

Although we don't know much about how Viking music sounded, we know they had whistles, harps, drums and panpipes.

Some Viking instruments have survived. This is a Viking whistle, made from a hollowed-out goose bone.

Writing messages

Those who could read and write amused themselves by writing each other short poems and messages. Viking people spoke a language that isn't used any more, called Old Norse, and wrote by carving letters, known as runes, into stone, bone or wood.

ᚠ ᚢ ᚦ ᚭ ᚱ ᚴ

F U TH A R K

ᚼ ᚾ ᛁ ᛅ ᛋ ᛏ ᛒ ᛘ ᛚ ᛦ

H N I A S T B M L R

The Viking alphabet is known as *futhark*, after the sounds of the first six runes. It consists of just 16 runes, made up of simple shapes and marks.

This is a copy of a Viking weaving tool from the 1100s. It has been inscribed with runes that read, "Think of me, I think of you! Love me, I love you! Have mercy on me!" It was probably given to a woman by her lovesick admirer.

GAMES

Viking men enjoyed playing board games to show off their skill. *Hnefatafl* (or 'King's Table'), a war game requiring great strategy, was the most common.

These Vikings are playing *Hnefatafl*, using a wooden board and playing pieces.

This carved wooden gaming board, dating from around 900, was probably used to play *Hnefatafl*. It is decorated with two wooden faces.

These blue glass playing pieces may have been used in *Hnefatafl*.

Dice games were popular, and could become very competitive. One game involved throwing the dice to see who gained the highest number.

These Viking dice are made from carved and polished bone.

Chess originated in India but, by around a thousand years ago, it had spread across most of Europe, and into the Viking lands.

These chess pieces were carved from walrus tusks and whale teeth in Norway around the year 1200. They are designed in the shape of Viking warriors, with pointed helmets and shields.

VIKING STORIES

The Vikings loved telling stories. From epic tales, called *sagas*, to dramatic poems, they told tales about real ancestors and kings, and mythical monsters, gods and heroes. Here are just a few of the most famous characters from the stories.

ERIK THE RED

One *saga* tells the story of explorer Erik the Red, who founded the first Viking settlement in Greenland. Erik had been banished from Iceland for murder, so he decided to sail to Greenland and explore the island.

LEIF ERIKSON

The *saga* about Erik the Red also tells of Erik's son, Leif Erikson, who is supposed to have sailed all the way to North America in the year 999, when he was blown off course on the way to Greenland.

CNUT THE GREAT

Court poets, called *skalds*, composed many poems in praise of Viking rulers. Cnut the Great – King of England, Denmark, Norway and parts of Sweden – was the subject of many poems.

Cnut's portrait appears on this English coin, made in around 1016.

This painting from around 1300 shows Cnut sitting proudly on his throne.

According to one poem, Cnut was told that he was so great, he could control the tides. But when he tried, he nearly drowned.

BRYNHILD

Brynhild was a mythical female warrior who appears in a story called the *Volsunga Saga*. She was said to be staggeringly beautiful, and admired for her skill and aggression in battle.

RAGNAR LOTHBROK

Ragnar's Saga tells the story of Ragnar Lothbrok, a legendary hero, who rescued a princess from a monstrous snake. He wore hairy leggings that protected him from the snake's poison.

IVAR RAGNARSSON

Ivar Ragnarsson was a real Viking leader, sometimes known as 'Ivar the Boneless'. Some people believe that he was unable to walk, as one story describes how he was carried around by his warriors on their shields.

ICELANDIC MANUSCRIPTS

Vikings living in Iceland were the first to write down the sagas and poems, around the year 1100. They wrote on sheets of parchment, made by stretching and smoothing the skins of sheep.

This is part of a collection of poems about gods and goddesses, known as the *Prose Edda*. It was first written around 800 years ago, but this copy was made around 200 years later.

The *Prose Edda* is thought to have been written down by a Viking poet from Iceland, named Snorri Sturluson.

END OF AN ERA

The Vikings were a force to be reckoned with for over 300 years. After that, times changed, and the beliefs and way of life of the Vikings gradually faded. But many objects and legends have survived, sometimes thanks to the Vikings' own customs.

DEATH AND REMEMBERING

Vikings believed in life after death, and buried and remembered their dead in distinctive ways. Sometimes, an important dead Viking was put in a ship along with prized possessions. Then, everything was burned and the ash buried.

Buried ashes can survive for centuries. Today, experts study them to find out more about Viking funerals and goods.

Some people set up tall stones in memory of their dead relatives. The stones usually had messages carved onto them in runes.

The runes on this stone show that it was a memorial set up by a father named Varinn for his dead son, Vamothr. Many characters from Viking legends are also mentioned.

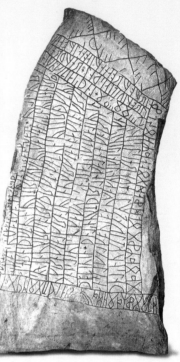

SHIP BURIALS

While some Vikings were burned in ships, others were buried in them. They were put in ships along with valuable possessions, and a mound of earth piled over the top. A few of these ships and their contents have been dug up in modern times.

This beautifully carved dragon head was found inside a burial ship at Oseberg in Norway.

Vikings may have believed that being buried in a ship enabled its occupant to sail off to the land of the dead – possibly Asgard.

TREASURE HOARDS

The Viking Age was an unsafe time when fighting was never far away. In times of particular danger, Vikings hid their valuables by burying them in the ground. Sometimes they never reclaimed them, and these stashes, known as hoards, were dug up centuries later.

A vast hoard of silver was dug up in 1840 at Cuerdale, in the north west of England. It had been carefully buried inside a lead chest.

This hoard was discovered in Hoen, Norway, in 1834. It includes gold coins, a beaded necklace and splendid gold rings.

THE RISE OF CHRISTIANITY

By the year 1050, near the end of the Viking Age, the Christian religion had arrived in Viking lands. It changed the Viking way of life forever, bringing new beliefs and customs. But these also left behind evidence that has survived to today.

This silver pendant is the oldest known crucifix in Sweden, dating from the 800s. It was found buried in a Viking grave.

Wooden churches were built all over the Viking lands, carved with both Christian crosses and traditional Viking dragon heads. Some of these churches, known as stave churches, are still standing today.

THE LAST RAIDS

As the Viking Age came to an end, the Vikings stopped raiding, as it became too hard and risky. Foreign kings now had well-trained armies to repel Viking attacks, and settlements were fortified with walls and ditches. But some of the last few Viking attacks became the stuff of legend.

In 1066, Harald Hardrada, King of Norway, led the last full-scale Viking attack on Europe when he tried to invade England, but was defeated at the Battle of Stamford Bridge. This painting of it was made 200 years later.

23

INDEX

Usborne Quicklinks

For links to websites where you can find out more about the Vikings, go to
www.usborne.com/quicklinks and type the keywords **Vikings picture book**.

Acknowledgements

Every effort has been made to trace and acknowledge ownership of copyright. If any rights have been omitted, the publishers offer to rectify this in any future editions following notification. The publishers are grateful to the following individuals and organizations for their permission to reproduce material on the following pages:

Cover: Coin © The Trustees of the British Museum; Helmet © Universitetets Oldsaksamling, University of Oslo, Norway, Photo © AISA/ The Bridgeman Art Library; Sword © The Trustees of the British Museum; Glass gaming pieces © Sören Hallgren/National Historical Museum, Stockholm, Sweden; Dragon head © Werner Forman Archive/Viking Ship Museum, Bygdoy.

p2-3 The Vikings: Dragon head © Werner Forman Archive/ Viking Ship Museum, Bygdoy; Gold box brooch © Ronald Sheridan @Ancient Art & Architecture Collection Ltd.

p4-5 Ships: Weather vane © The Art Archive/Alamy; Anchor © Werner Forman Archive; Ship © Werner Forman Archive/Bergen Maritime Museum; Manuscript © 2013. Photo Pierpont Morgan Library/Art Resource/Scala, Florence; Coin © Werner Forman Archive/Statens Historiska Museum, Stockholm.

p6-7 Battle gear: Sword © The Trustees of the British Museum; Short axe © Gary Ombler/Dorling Kindersley/Getty Images; Long axe © Dorling Kindersley/Getty Images; Sax and scabbard © Jinx Photography/Alamy; Shield © Andy Crawford/Dorling Kindersley/Getty Images; Tapestry © Photos 12/Alamy; Conical helmet © Andy Crawford/Dorling Kindersley/Getty Images; Helmet with spectacles © Universitetets Oldsaksamling, University of Oslo, Norway, Photo © AISA/The Bridgeman Art Library.

p8-9 The Viking world: Sledge © Museum of Cultural History - University of Oslo, Norway Photographer: Eirik Irgens Johnsen, UiO/ CC BY-SA 4.0; Cart/wagon p.8-9 © Museum of Cultural History - University of Oslo, Norway Photographer: Eirik Irgens Johnsen, UiO/ CC BY-SA 4.0.

p10-11 At home: Iron pots © Viking Ship Museum, Oslo, Norway/Giraudon/The Bridgeman Art Library; Drinking horn © Photo by: Christer Åhlin/National Historical Museum, Stockholm, Sweden; Reconstruction of bed © Museum of Cultural History - University of Oslo, Norway Photographer: Kojan & Krogvold, UiO/ CC BY-SA 4.0; Smoothing board © The Trustees of the British Museum; Comb © The Trustees of the British Museum.

p12-13 Ornaments: Beads (right) © Photo by: Gabriel Hildebrand/National Historical Museum, Stockholm, Sweden; Beads (left) © Photo by: Christer Åhlin/National Historical Museum, Stockholm, Sweden; Gold brooches © Nationalmuseet, Copenhagen, Denmark/The Bridgeman Art Library; Silver ring pin © Ronald Sheridan @ Ancient Art & Architecture Collection Ltd.; Arm ring and finger ring © Photo by Ulf Bruxe/ National Historical Museum, Stockholm, Sweden; Thor pendant © Werner Forman Archive/ Statens Historiska Museum, Stockholm; Crystal necklace © Christer Åhlin/National Historical Museum, Stockholm, Sweden; Casket © Werner Forman Archive/National Museum, Copenhagen.

p14-15 Crafts and trade: Axe head © Werner Forman Archive/National Museum, Copenhagen, Sweden; Metalworking tools © York Archaeological Trust 2013; Scales © Werner Forman Archive/University Museum of National Antiquities, Uppsala, Sweden; Hacksilver © Museum of Cultural History - University of Oslo, Norway, Photographer: Eirik Irgens Johnsen, UiO/ CC BY-SA 4.0; Glass cup © Gunnel Jansson/National Historical Museum, Stockholm, Sweden; Shoes © York Archaeological Trust 2013.

p18-19 Pastimes: Glass drinking cup © Gabriel Hildebrand/National Historical Museum, Stockholm, Sweden; Whistle © York Archaeological Trust 2013; Weaving tool © National Historical Museum, Stockholm, Sweden; Wooden gaming board © National Museum of Ireland, Dublin, Ireland, Photo © Boltin Picture Library/The Bridgeman Art Library; Glass gaming pieces © Sören Hallgren/National Historical Museum, Stockholm, Sweden; Dice © York Archaeological Trust 2013; Lewis chess pieces © The Trustees of the British Museum.

p20-21 Viking stories: Cnut manuscript © akg-images/British Library; Coin © The Trustees of the British Museum; Prose Edda © Werner Forman Archive/Universitetetsbiblioteket, Uppsala, Sweden.

p22-23 End of an era: Rune stone © INTERFOTO/Alamy; Dragon head © Werner Forman Archive/Viking Ship Museum, Bygdoy; The Hoen Hoard © Viking Ship Museum, Oslo, Norway/Giraudon/The Bridgeman Art Library; Silver crucifix © Gabriel Hildebrand/National Historical Museum, Stockholm, Sweden; The Life of Edward the Confessor by Matthew Paris, Ee.3.59 f. 31 recto, Reproduced by kind permission of the Syndics of Cambridge University Library.

Edited by Abigail Wheatley

With thanks to Ruth King   Digital manipulation by John Russell and Nick Wakeford

First published in 2016 by Usborne Publishing Ltd., Usborne House, 83-85 Saffron Hill, London, EC1N 8RT, England.

To Christopher,
with love
  ~ T.K.

For David
  ~ H.O.

First published 2016 by Walker Books Ltd, 87 Vauxhall Walk, London SE11 5HJ

10 9 8 7 6 5 4 3 2 1

Text © 2016 Timothy Knapman
Illustrations © 2016 Helen Oxenbury

The right of Timothy Knapman and Helen Oxenbury to be identified as author
and illustrator respectively of this work has been asserted by them in accordance
with the Copyright, Designs and Patents Act 1988

This book has been typeset in Bodoni Egyptian Pro

Printed in Italy

British Library Cataloguing in Publication Data:
a catalogue record for this book is available from the British Library

ISBN 978-1-4063-6735-5

www.walker.co.uk

Time Now to Dream

Timothy Knapman   *illustrated by* Helen Oxenbury

WALKER BOOKS
AND SUBSIDIARIES
LONDON · BOSTON · SYDNEY · AUCKLAND

Alice and Jack were out
playing catch when they heard
something that sounded like...

Ocka by hay beees
unna da reeees

"What's that noise?" said Jack.

"It's coming from the forest,"
  said Alice. "Let's go and see!"

"But what if it's the Wicked Wolf?"
  said Jack. "I want to go home."

"Shhh," said Alice.
"Everything is going to be all right."

    And she held Jack's hand.

Alice and Jack were stepping into the forest when they heard something that sounded like…

Offtis or eeef edd un gentil daa breeze

"What's that noise?" said Jack.
"I don't like it."

"Let's go and see," said Alice.

"But what if it's the Wicked Wolf,"
  said Jack, "with his big bad claws?"

"Shhh," said Alice.
"Everything is going to be all right."

Alice and Jack were creeping through the forest when they heard something that sounded like…

I me now to reem ing de taaars in a sky

"What's that noise?" said Jack.
"We're lost!"

"It's just over there," said Alice.
"Let's go and see."

"What if it's the Wicked Wolf,"
said Jack, "with his big bad claws
and his snap-trap jaws?"

"Shhh," said Alice.
"Everything is going to be all right."

"I want to be home," said Jack.

"I want to be warm and wearing my pyjamas.
I want to be snuggled down deep."

"We have to be brave," said Alice.

And that's when they heard it,
very close now.

Sossay to leeep
on mie eeeet ullaby

"It's right in front of us!"
said Jack.

Big bad claws ...
snap-trap jaws ...

THE WICKED WOLF!

"RUN!" cried Alice.

"All the way home!"

But Jack didn't move.

"The Wolf isn't wicked," said Jack.
"The Wolf is a mummy…
That's what the noise is!
Wolf Mummy is singing her babies
to sleep!

Look!"

Rock-a-bye babies
under the trees,

Soft is your leaf bed
and gentle the breeze,

Time now to dream
sing the stars in the sky,

So sail off to sleep
on my sweet lullaby.

"Everything is all right," said Jack.
Then he gave a great big yawn.
"It's time to go home."

And he held Alice's hand.

Alice and Jack
walked back through
the forest ...

and all the way home.

They got into their
nice, warm pyjamas and
snuggled down deep.

And they sailed off to sleep
on that sweet lullaby.